Whispering to Fool the Wind

Winner of the Walt Whitman Award for 1981

Sponsored by The Academy of American Poets, the Walt Whitman Award is given annually to the winner of an open competition among American poets who have not yet published a first book of poems.

Judge for 1981: Donald Justice

ACKNOWLEDGMENTS

Academy of American Poets: Selections (1973-78): "Mi Abuelo." AMERICAN LITERARY REVIEW: "The Purpose of Altar Boys." THE BILINGUAL REVIEW/LA REVISTA BILINGUE: "Deciding on a Face." CEDAR ROCK: "The Man Who Became Old," "The Man She Called Honey, and Married," "Spring in the Only Place Spring Was," "Afternoon," "Grandfather, They Say, Sang." CUTBANK: "The Man Who Named Children," "Lost on September Trail, 1967." *A Geography of Poets:* "Nani." THE GREYLEDGE REVIEW: "The Other Calendar." HIGH COUNTRY NEWS: "Sonoita Burn." THE IOWA REVIEW: "Winter Along the Santa Cruz." IRONWOOD: "The Man I Cannot Talk To," "The Man With Two Canes," "Madre Sofía," "Camp of the Third Night." THE LITTLE MAGAZINE: "The Arroyo, Sergio, and Me." LOST GLOVE: "Wet Camp." THE LOUISVILLE REVIEW: "Mi Abuelo." MANGO: "Sundays Visiting." MAGAZINE: "Palomino." MOUNTAIN NEWSREAL: "The Pioneer Hotel Fire." EL NAHUATZEN: "Mayates." NORTH AMERICAN REVIEW: "Returning to the Cat." PEARL: "The Man Who Has Waited, Not Out of Patience." PORCH: "Kino Viejo." REVISTA CHICANO-RIQUEÑA: "Some Years," "The Woman's Ears." A SHOUT IN THE STREET: "Belita." *Southwest: A Contemporary Anthology:* "Nani." THE SPIRIT THAT MOVES US: "Morning," "El Molino Rojo." WATERS: "La Sequía." A number of these poems have also appeared in two earlier chapbooks: *Sleeping on Fists* and *Elk Heads on the Wall.*

I owe thanks also to the National Endowment for the Arts and the Arizona Commission on the Arts for grants of financial assistance during the years many of these poems were written, to my friends who have given me their encouragement and support, and special thanks to Donald Justice, Michael Cuddihy, Stanley Moss, and the Academy of American Poets.

WHISPERING
TO FOOL THE WIND

poems by

Alberto Ríos

The Sheep Meadow Press
New York

All inquiries and permission requests should be addressed to:
The Sheep Meadow Press, Post Office Box 1345,
Riverdale-on-Hudson, New York 10471.

Distributed by: The Sheep Meadow Press.

Printed on acid-free paper in the United States. This book meets the guidelines for permanence and durability of the Committee on Production Guidelines for Book Longevity of the Council on Library Resources.

Library of Congress Cataloging-in-Publication Data:

Ríos, Alberto
        Whispering to fool the wind
                p.   cm.
            ISBN 0-935296-31-X
            1. Title.
        PS3568.I587W5
        811'.54   82-3269
                                                              CIP

Cover drawing by Francesco Salviati

Second Printing 1994

For this friend, Lupita

You see there are in our countries rivers which have no names, trees which nobody knows, and birds which nobody has described.... Our duty, then, as we understand it, is to express what is unheard of.

—Pablo Neruda

Contents

Whispering to Fool the Wind

Lost on September Trail, 1967

There was a roof over our heads
and that was at least something.
Then came dances.
The energy for them came from
childhood, or before, from the time
when only warmth was important.
We had come to the New World
and become part of it.
If the roof would shelter us,
we would keep it in repair.
Roof then could be roof,
solid, visible, recognizable,
and we could be whatever it was
that we were at this moment.
Having lost our previous names
somewhere in the rocks as we ran,
we could not yet describe ourselves.
For two days the rain had been
steady, and we left the trail
because one of us remembered
this place. Once when I was young
I had yielded to the temptation
of getting drunk, and parts of it
felt like this, wet and hot,
timeless, in the care of someone
else. After the dances we sat
like cubs, and cried for that
which in another world might be
milk, but none came.
We had only ourselves, side by side
and we began a wrestling
that comes, like dances, out of

nowhere and leaves into the night
like sophisticated daughters
painted and in plumes, but young,
a night darker than its name.
We gave ourselves over to adoration
of the moon, but we did not call it
moon, the words that came out
were instead noises as we tried
to coax it close enough
to where we might jump,
overpower it, and bring it to our
mouths, which is, after all,
the final test of all things.
But we could not, it only circled us,
calmly, and we wanted it more.
We called it Carlos, but it did not
come, we called it friend, comrade,
but nothing. We used every word
until we fell, exhausted, and slept
with our eyes open, not trusting
each other, dark pushing us even
farther into childhood, into liquid,
making us crave eyelessness,
craving so hard we understand
prayer without knowing its name.
At some point failing
ourselves, eyelids fell.
We dreamt the dreams of farther
worlds, so different they cannot
be remembered, cannot be remembered
because they cannot be described
or even imagined. We woke
and did not remember, and the night
before became part of us
and we did not remember

4

speaking to the moon.
We got up from the years without numbers
and called
each other by name.
Honey, the one that was me said,
drying her tears that were
really the rain from the night
before, which had taken her
without me knowing, *honey*,
again, but she did not understand.
She wanted only the sun
because she was cold, she pulled out
hair to offer it, from her head
and her arms. She understood me
only when I held her, made her
warm. She reached to her head
and offered now me
more of herself. I took it.
I put it to my mouth,
put it to a cupped tongue
and took it in. She moved
and I put my hands on her knees
which looked up at opposite ends
of the sky.

The Man Who Named Children

Panfilo's head was shaped awkwardly
so that his mother would let out
one side of his hat.
He prayed for himself
and confessed this, finally
to the priest, Father Torres
who recognized Panfilo's voice
in the confessional and said
it was all right.
The priest was there
when Panfilo was born,
when his mother almost died
and needed extreme unction.
Panfilo remembered being scared.
He was taken wrapped in a blanket
to his father who wanted a son.
But this is ugly! said his father
holding him up by the lightbulb
so the other men could see.
I will name him Panfilo
he decided, and from my corner
I remember seeing
as the men looked down
at their hands and said
to Panfilo's father yes,
each in his turn.

True Story of the Pins

Pins are always plentiful
but one day they were not
and your Uncle Humberto,
who collected all the butterflies
you see here on the walls,
was crazy looking for some
and he went to your cousin
Graciela the hard seamstress
who has pins it is rumored
even in hard times
but when she found out
why he wanted them
because the wind from the south
who was her friend
since the days of her
childhood on the sea
told her, she firmly refused
your poor Uncle Humberto
whose picture is here
on the wall behind you,
did you feel his eyes,
and he went into the most terrible
of rages, too terrible
for a butterfly collector
we all said afterward
and he burst the vein
that grew like a great snake
on his small forehead
and he died on the dirt
floor of Graciela's house
who of course felt sick
and immediately went

and put pins, this is what has
made her hard, through
the bright wings of the butterflies
Humberto had prepared
since he was after all
her father and she
could afford no better
light of perpetuity.

Belita

The faces and the hands of her grandchildren
had grown too big to fit through her eyes.
She learned to keep bowed her head
because fingers and ankles she could recognize
and faces she could not, not even her own
which fit her now like a wrinkled handkerchief,

like the brown, unlaundered, unironed handkerchief
she kept always in her hands because her grandchildren
had given it to her, had allowed her to own
some part of them, a larger part than her eyes
would have allowed; she could recognize
in her hands the face from her head

better than in a mirror, and her head
felt lighter without eyes, or ears, and the handkerchief
she massaged constantly showed her how to recognize
clearly why not one of her grandchildren
would touch her; she could feel their eyes
also with her fingers, and they were like her own,

afraid of looking, and their lips were like her own,
afraid of speaking, and she was kissed only on the forehead
because of this, and with her fingers that were eyes
she felt afraid, again, again, crushing the handkerchief
because these were the children of her children
and in them she could not fail to recognize

herself, trying nervously, trembling, not to recognize
death, how it had taken her name, Belita, for its own.
She remembered her friends suddenly as children,
how they had played Death like this because ahead

only dinner waited for them, how each took a handkerchief
and pulled it slowly over the mouth, the nose, the eyes.

Now it was her turn, and quickly her own eyes
closed; in her short life she had learned to recognize
how a sheet was like a handkerchief
and how both could be her own, and yet not her own,
how each covered easily the length of her head,
how the pennies put on her eyes balanced like children.

But those eyes are not her own.
She cannot recognize any longer the little head,
covered now by that handkerchief, kissed by the children.

At Kino Viejo, Mexico

The potatoes of the corner store sing,
sand crickets and green flies full,
fat almost like night beetles,
the burlap bags of dry onions move,
the loose copper skins jumping
to the wild *sandunga* dance
brought by rich gypsies from the south
two summers previous, jumping
like the rhythms of the flat yellow
grandmother fingers, always knitting
for a birth, fingers husbandless
and almost quiet in the outer room
with the Bible and the picture.
Inside, on all the cool black nights
the young men are making love
privately with two of the older women
whose long flower names are known
and whose families are shamed.
No one speaks about nature;
here it is a private pain.
The children go naked in the dirt
and have red coughs.
Over the hills the ocean, once
seen, once touched, is of use to no one
but the gypsies who returned
to the south with parts of it to sell;
the fish of the bay, the sharks
and the white lisa, were all caught
one summer, the year of the fat August.
It is the job of four elected men
to keep the sand from the ocean

away, but they cannot.
Rumored widely not to have weeds,
scared away by the great animal sounds
of the ocean, coming closer at night,
weeds are the lie of this town.

Morning

He cradled his head in those hands
which might have kept it,
which might have grown into part of his head
but I would come in, and call him, *daddy*,
and they would let go.
Every day I saw a man
who wore one suit
and had a beard hid under his skin.
It was black.
I could see it in the light
see its darkness
as it came out first through his eyes
precisely in their centers
when he looked at me.
Under his suit, under his shirt
and undershirt, it started coming
through his chest too, and on his back.
He thought about his beard
because it was tangled in his head.
It made him unhappy,
his head was heavy
and sometimes he rested it in those hands
letting his beard come out through
their backs, through the backs
of his palms, the backs of his fingers,
through the backs of things lost.

Carlos

Carlos is the name
by which loneliness
knows each of us.
Carlos the distant relative
worse off than we are
drank the medicines
of poverty and died
not in his sleep
but wide awake
clutching the red chair
because alone
his most powerful act
was this.
Carlos who lives inside
pain in each of us
knowing one woman,
it was her brother that died
and that was all,
he was dead
and everyone was sorry
because her hands
were too heavy to lift.
Carlos at this moment
wanting desperately other women
looking out through my eyes
making my tongue his
speaking my words
hearing his meanings.
Carlos who is the name of a boat
and the fishermen and the anchor.
Carlos who is the cold

and the women and the night.
Carlos who wants only
to age with each of us,
to grow old, to be happy.

Why Animals Stay Away

An owl landed in a tree
next to the house
and spoke to me
in its language
which is comforting
like the second language
of mothers who are divorced
and have children.
I called back to the owl
using its human name,
but it did not come.
I called it Carlos,
but nothing.
I tried to speak
its language, but I
could not. The distance
in between us
was a third animal.

Afternoon

She didn't raise her head for so many years
she forgot all about the sky.
Suspicions grew about the woman
who wore her purse close like an arm
in a third black sleeve.
But when she sat one afternoon
to wait for death in the plaza
she remembered the sky like her husband.
She waited. She did not look up.
Her intimacy now was with the night
and it slipped into her
and wore her like a sleeve.

The Man Who Became Old

For every year, he grew a new tooth
and this, at least among his friends,
created around him a kind of fame,
but the kind that everyone gets used to
so that it was only occasionally enjoyable.
And his mouth kept getting bigger
or really, his jawbone, so that he
began taking on the aspect of a wolf
though roughly his teeth were equally sized.
And then it came that he was forty-five
and spent his nights still unmarried.
He looked now like the old cartoon wolf
in a zoot suit flipping a coin and whistling,
and his friends all abandoned him.
He could barely remember them.
With each new tooth, a friend left,
the same way that in the early days
a friend came, so that for fifteen years, now
he was alone, and could find no work.
People ran when he walked the streets
so he stayed in his apartment
almost entirely, and ordered take-out.
His friends said it was better this way,
then remembered they were no longer
friends, that it didn't matter.
He dreamed about the half-dressed tooth fairy
every night, and finally she took him.

The Man With Two Canes

The shoehorn refuses to work.
Things are like that now.
A man has two canes in his hands
because he is old
not because he is fierce.
He uses two canes to walk
because one will no longer do
and because he is not yet dead,
still dreaming of the other man
plainly, sitting or asleep
in a chair inside himself, bored,
that other man everyday shot sleeping
through the heel up straight
through the leg, bullet
stopping, probably, somewhere.
The man jumps out of his chair,
stands on his heel to stop the blood,
wet spot at his crotch
as if from there he were bleeding
the real pain of the wound.
Which man jumped he doesn't know,
himself, or the man inside,
but it will happen again tomorrow,
it will happen or he will imagine it,
the same way he knows
the young men are leaving here
and the young women were never young
and never wore tee-shirts
that let their ninnies show.

The Man Who Has Waited,
Not Out of Patience

The eagles came
from out of the night
pulling me from my room
with their beaks.
They carried me
to the cut
northern edge
of the dream,
to the place I could touch
membrane sides,
and waiting for me
was the pock-faced man
whose marks I had seen
in all the parts of this place.
Always his was the farm
without sound.
Always his were the cows
allowed dead on the road
green flies sticking
in the exposed nostril.
This is the man
who had grown once
so angry
his look had terrified
even the harvest.
And that look was in him now
sucking his face
to a single wrinkle
so deep it drew
and drew me with the strength
of metal toward its slippery

fenceless edge one puppet step
and another, until I fell
quickly and easily upward
with all the helium
balloons of my life, falling
to the edge of the well of the eye.
Inside him, him who is
my grandfather dead before we touched,
him whose picture hangs
on the face of my grandmother,
on her hands, on her hair, her walls,
inside him, stopped,
frozen in scream's middle,
were all the children
that have ever been lost.
I called to them,
and my mouth stopped.

Mi Abuelo

Where my grandfather is is in the ground
where you can hear the future
like a movie Indian with his ear at the tracks.
A pipe leads down to him so that sometimes
he whispers what will happen to a man
in town or how he will meet the best
dressed woman tomorrow and how the best
man at her wedding will chew the ground
next to her. Mi abuelo is the man
who speaks through all the mouths in my house.
An echo of me hitting the pipe sometimes
to stop him from saying *my hair is a*
sieve is the only other sound. It is a phrase
that among all others is the best,
he says, and *my hair is a sieve* is sometimes
repeated for hours out of the ground
when I let him, which is not often.
An abuelo should be much more than a man
like you! He stops then, and speaks: *I am a man*
who has served ants with the attitude
of a waiter, who has made each smile as only
an ant who is fat can, and they liked me best,
but there is nothing left. Yet I know he ground
green coffee beans as a child, and sometimes
he will talk about his wife, and sometimes
about when he was deaf and a man
cured him by mail and he heard groundhogs
talking, or about how he walked with a cane
he chewed on when he got hungry.
At best, mi abuelo is a liar.
I see an old picture of him at nani's with an
off-white yellow center mustache and sometimes

that's all I know for sure. He talks best
about these hills, *slowest waves*, and where this man
is going, and I'm convinced his hair is a sieve,
that his fever is cooled now underground.
Mi abuelo is an ordinary man.
I look down the pipe, sometimes, and see a
ripple-topped stream in its best suit, in the ground.

Mayates

Take thread any color
the length of yourself,
fold open the june bug's wings
with pressure on its stomach
and hold them open with
your left index finger, thumb
and middle finger around the sides,
and tie the thread up under
its wings, around the body,
not too tight but not so easy
it'll slip right out.
The legs won't hurt;
don't pull them off, or
just the forelegs, they're strongest.
Hold tight and blow
on its eyes to make it
flap its wings and
if it does you're ready.
Tie the loose thread end around
your right index finger.
Stand outside or in the biggest
part of the living room
and twirl it around your head
like a sling shot until it flies.
It'll zoom around in circles
as long as you stand there
if you jerk when
it tries to land.
At night, tie it to the door knob
and it'll sleep.

Madre Sofía

My mother took me because she couldn't
wait the second ten years to know.
This was the lady rumored to have been
responsible for the box-wrapped baby
among the presents at that wedding,
but we went in, anyway, through the curtains.
Loose jar-top, half turned
and not caught properly in the threads
her head sat mimicking its original intention
like the smile of a child hitting himself.
Central in that head grew unfamiliar poppies
from a face mahogany, eyes half yellow
half gray at the same time, goat and fog,
slit eyes of the devil, his tweed suit, red
lips, and she smelled of smoke, cigarettes,
but a diamond smoke, somehow; I inhaled
sparkles, I could feel them, throat, stomach.
She did not speak, and as a child
I could only answer, so that together
we were silent, cold and wet, dry and hard:
from behind my mother pushed me forward.
The lady put her hand on the face
of a thin animal wrap, tossing that head
behind her to be pressured incredibly
as she sat back in the huge chair and leaned.
And then I saw the breasts as large as her
head, folded together, coming out of her dress
as if it didn't fit, not like my mother's.
I could see them, how she kept them
penned up, leisurely, in maroon feed bags,
horse nuzzles of her wide body,
but exquisitely penned up

circled by pearl reins and red scarves.
She lifted her arm, but only with the tips
of her fingers motioned me to sit opposite.
She looked at me but spoke to my mother
words dark, smoky like the small room,
words coming like red ants stepping occasionally
from a hole on a summer day in the valley,
red ants from her mouth, her nose, her ears,
tears from the corners of her cinched eyes.
And suddenly she put her hand full on my head
pinching tight again with those finger tips
like a television healer, young Oral Roberts
half standing, quickly, half leaning
those breasts swinging toward me
so that I reach with both my hands to my lap
protecting instinctively whatever it is
that needs protection when a baseball is thrown
and you're not looking but someone yells,
the hand, then those breasts coming toward me
like the quarter-arms of the amputee Joaquín
who came back from the war to sit
in the park, reaching always for children
until one day he had to be held back.
I sat there, no breath, and could see only
hair around her left nipple, like a man.
Her clothes were old.
Accented, in a language whose spine had been
snapped, she whispered the words of a city
witch, and made me happy, alive like a man:
The future will make you tall.

Spring in the Only Place Spring Was

At twelve I remember jumping
in and out of the several open graves
onto the cool lawn here that was green
and shaved, like nothing else in Arizona,
ten, fifty, a hundred of us
crazy like canes
old men lift dresses with,
the two of us running
so fast we'd never get caught,
running through a hundred lives
with our feet
and only our feet have grown old
so that now we look down
and wonder whose they are.

The Purpose of Altar Boys

Tonio told me at catechism
the big part of the eye
admits good, and the little
black part is for seeing
evil—his mother told him
who was a widow and so
an authority on such things.
That's why at night
the black part gets bigger.
That's why kids can't go out
at night, and at night
girls take off their clothes
and walk around their
bedrooms or jump on their
beds or wear only sandals
and stand in their windows.
I was the altar boy
who knew about these things,
whose mission on some Sundays
was to remind people of
the night before as they
knelt for Holy Communion.
To keep Christ from falling
I held the metal plate
under chins, while on the thick
red carpet of the altar
I dragged my feet
and waited for the precise
moment: plate to chin
I delivered without expression
the Holy Electric Shock,
the kind that produces

a really large swallowing
and makes people think.
I thought of it as justice.
But on other Sundays the fire
in my eyes was different,
my mission somehow changed.
I would hold the metal plate
a little too hard
against those certain same
nervous chins, and I
I would look
with authority down
the tops of white dresses.

The Arroyo, Sergio, and Me

We went in that arroyo just to cuss
down everything and everyone to mud
at least a hundred times and maybe worse
because we could, just that, because we could

and no one ever said a thing to us,
not even when we screamed for teacher blood
those summer afternoons of *go to hell,*
of maim and rape and Claudia and kill.

So boy! was that one heck of a you bet! place,
and what we found there, me and him, was swell,
the swellest, underneath that rotting brace
of railroad bridge: a rounded, solid, dull

and beautiful steel ball the Southern P.,
who'd blow their whistle if they saw you call,
had used for ballast maybe, or bombs —
what do caboose men do when they get bored?

We buried it, cause it was perfect; it
was all we talked about, till we forgot.

Sonoita Burn

The town is still far off,
it's the wind that brings it close.
Eventually night comes
and the talcum ashes rise.
Smoke fills my eyes
making tears like thick glasses
and the town fires far off
are the last thing I see
before I curl to sleep and dream
of a new sky covering me
whose million sparks are more alive,
and the black, where the fire has been.

Camp of the Third Night

The green apples fall hollow and flat
picked out by the sparrows
like the bulbous eyes of fat men who have
sinned so that their graves are left
shallow, obvious and mounded up
for the animals of all worlds.
Together we catch the night of this place
forcing it into our bodies.
We dream of evil sounds
but mine are the worst, I dream of
the apples, of the origins of hollowness,
and wake to repeat their unfortunate story
taking everything in from the imagination
of the earth, leaving its parts dry,
its continents and rivers
its names and thousand meridians, dry
like the texture of a library globe,
until this fat story of the apples
becomes more real than anything
we can remember as we lie
on our spines under the visible faces
of the sparrows in the trees, feeling
inside the moving feast of the black.

Palomino

He's dead now,
town drunk like a witch
who is really a whore
everybody yelling obscenities
and palming him money
the right to yell again tomorrow
at his thousand filthy hats
all gifts
of a small town searching
for a soccer team
that will kick your balls off
or grab them and pull
finding everything connected
mysteriously to the tongue.
Nothing left of Mr. Palomino
no insides
when a man lies in bed
and lets his cigarette burn
into his fingers
because it doesn't hurt
as much as the rest of him.
Mama, he said to the nurse
who was, mama, this time.
Ay, Palomino, again.
What was left to smile with
he moved
the smart of his lip breaking
more times, more places
because that was all
because that was left undone
the only job
left to make them proud

hijos de la chingada.
I saw Mr. Palomino last.
Did I go to the bathroom?
I told him yes
and he nodded his head.

Returning to the Cat

The most obscene places of all
are the undersides of bridges
sprayed with Y's and UU's
and a child's greatest
I WAS HERE and a child's
cruelest *Robert loves Raul.*
Here I have passed for the fourth time
the cat whose careful movements
and sliced marble eyes follow me.
Because I am a man
I have known it is exactly a cat
without looking into its dirtsheet bed.
But today I stop, and come back;
its movements are as cautious as mine,
like an old puppet's
whose rotting strings
must be pulled up gently,
as it explains carefully to me
the secrets of the ground underneath,
its body and separate fur crowded
with filled maggots and living things
squirming with ideas like
a child's body on a church pew.
Patches, I think, is buried
under the thin peach tree
and Susie under my brother's window.
Weasel just never came home.
And my grandfather.
From then, the mudhole
at every step is frightening
as if the ground instead were coming up,
my feet not going down,

and whistling doesn't help
so that I must come back
a fifth and a sixth day and more
to this halfblack world underneath
to alter my new knowledge
because I can't live with it,
feeling better even
by being more frightened each time
as, like the cat might have,
the smell follows me home.

Scraping the Grate

When I clean out the fireplace
more than ashes resist.
Like the particles rising in
a fist, I think of another fire
taller than four of us
one night as we walked around,
or pictures of the Pioneer Hotel
burning, an older couple holding
hands as they jumped and jumped
as only a photograph allows.
But finally I rest on adolescence
as a reason for cleaning now.
These are the semen ash
that are the construction materials
for depression, the residue
after flames inside a new body,
body like a covered garbage can
in which a spray paint tin has
exploded. In my hands I hold
now a small broom; in the black
pieces of finished fire,
in the years candled, the places
felt, again I have a new body,
the same one, also grown blacker.
When I clean out the fireplace
more than ashes resist
the clean and absolute test
of moving from one place.

The Midnight Show

The trick was
she used eight veils.
No one had explained to her
art, commitment,
truth in advertising,
simple human decency.
Or that all dancers want
to be suddenly naked,
and that everyone wants
to be a dancer at midnight,
stretching a thin body
into the distances beyond
this building, the places
without Christian names,
didn't she understand this?
To have wind in my legs,
water in my arms,
to lose the sense of *hands*.
To be a man whose sex
derives from descriptions
in a junior high lockerroom,
to be a woman whose breasts
could shuck corn
if required to.
Everything farther
and stronger and lighter
than possible, in a single
taut turning stretch and lean
until exhaustion comes
honestly, with honest sleep.
But she keeps covered,

this girl I've been watching.
I shake my head.
I can think only to say
amateur, amateur.

The Other Calendar

Each of us wants only
a beautiful new girl
and a motorcycle,
unfamiliar breasts
riding on our backs.
We ride outside
of memory and order,
ride faster, shake
fists at the road
behind us. We forget
our names and attach
to ourselves only
beautiful faces.
Today is Saturday
regardless of the
calendar, morning,
early, wide awake
in tight jeans,
purposeful but without
plan. Each of us
wants only a chance
to feel in his hands
the morning
of this eighth day,
the real Saturday
whose name has been
fraudulently used.

One Night in a Familiar Room

Swinging his arm the way children do
body plugged with beer and plantains
he had begun to complain about something
sounding like the death of a cousin.
He afforded that cousin many gestures,
happy himself to be alive and able
to pantomime a choking from lemon pits.
But then he erased the scene
pulling his coatsleeve over his hand
and polishing the air free.
One August morning in the mine, he began
again, where mornings were left to rumor
another cousin choked from spiritual
possession wearing the insidious clothes
of blackened dust, he shook and he shook
like a Fundamentalist on a good night.
And then he stopped his imitation.
It is a simple thing, he said,
and mentioned the name of Hannibal.
He could discuss such men
for he had once been a student
and had worn a younger body.
The General crossed the Alps.
He came from war and he went to war.
Everything in between was a struggle.
This night in the familiar room
each of his friends spoke to him
and tried to take him home, and he agreed
in every case. His beers were gone
and his beers were gone.

El Molino Rojo

In this country, in one small town
many wooden buildings stand even today,
one of which is a bar
with elk heads on the wall
and half-empty long bottles on the shelves
but where is served
only a sick man's lunch
because the men who used to
drink beer have grown
old like the wood.
The bar closes at five, sometimes earlier
and no one fights
now that the women are old, too.
The men come every day.

Cuate is the fat twin
who never met his brother,
the baby that was buried
home near the row of mesquites
by the river, high enough so no one worries.
He still has a good job
only mornings now
but doing what he has always done.
The man's dark lips move,
he tries to recall his own childhood
the bugs, the smell of anise
of mint in the side garden after watering,
the smell of wet sand in the wash,
in his feet, on his legs.
He sniffs for a moment
gets only soup
the pepper slap to his nose

but glad to eat it
to stop floating
to let it make him heavy again.
He grabs the spoon, forgets the napkin,
how much he wants to live,
quietly, his lips say.

Robles sits only in one place,
the place he fought for
and says he must have
but doesn't explain.
He frowns, watching how
Cuate's lips always move,
frowns even at his beer
which is soup, but mysterious.
No one believes him
but no one is sure.
He stops frowning
and this is the signal to listen:
dirty fingernails are salty.
The women he has had.
The pulque, sometimes,
to make it better, in the south,
the Indians, they....
With his right hand,
fingers like they hold and weigh a pencil,
he makes an up-and-down motion
next to his crotch.
He nods, it's true, into the pulque.
Then he frowns again
busy with a colored toothpick
and sucking his teeth.

Indio shines shoes in the barber shop

there, across the street
even though he is not Black.
But the Blacks are his friends,
permanently bruised
so that their faces are always swollen.
He says he will soon look like them
ugly but hard, armadillos.
He will live for centuries
because he deserves to.
Everyone agrees.
His job must guarantee him
at least this.
Proud and a man,
the best pool player,
Indio belongs here,
Chapo's arm around his shoulders,
Cuate betting,
where everyone ignores
sick stomach, weak legs.

Chapo is the youngest
who died two years ago
but still must come here
because he has nowhere else
and no one.
He is always popular
telling the jokes of a drunk,
sometimes in a girl's voice,
silly, but only out of habit.
He no longer drinks
and each is glad,
they've been telling him for so long.
A shudder comes over him:
misfortune is near.
No one listens to him

because he is dead,
but each man thinks,
what can he mean.

Missy comes because he is the owner.
His wife died
who knew how to say no,
how to get money from those who had none,
and now he will have to close this place
but will never tell these men.
They will always come here
because they have to,
whose favorite joke is the broken pool table,
told over and over again,
dirty like he imagines Robles' pulque
but he can't do anything to fix it
even when they ask sometimes without laughing.
He wants to
or he wants to be able to tell the men
to go somewhere else
and go with them.
Let someone else be Missy,
someone with a wife.

A Boy's Jacket Gets in His Way

At night, the sound of a siren feels like
the pumping lead foot
of a tired bicyclist uphill.
I kissed you once, so my tongue
hurt every morning.
Mouth-aware like scat singers
we desired nothing else in each other
dividing the last minute
into halves and halves.
True weavers, I've heard,
corrugated their fingernails
to separate their threads more easily
and then a child was born with ridges
who remembers pushing his fingernail
down the wax of the Shamrock milk carton
feeling it collect like
on the cement steps of the stadium
I put a finger into you
like I was looking for something
and wiped it on my jeans.
And later I used enough fingers
for a fist, as if I were
putting something there instead.

At night, her little toe makes no longer
any attempt to curve inward.
This anniversary comes, inherited
as from weavers but more vulnerable.
Fat girls, I whisper, can have no morals.
I face away from her, stop talking to her
knowing she has slept
this whole time in the smell

of what a day is on my skin.
Tomorrow she will be married to a man
who, one Sunday, slugs
the large bowl of potato salad
to feel its give, nothing more
the simple first sound
of a hot new language.
A new word will be born like a child
and she'll feel it biting at her nipple
fling it to the ground
examining the corrugated scratches
on her heavy white skin.
And later, like the word he scratched
as a child in the confessional
his absence, clearly, will name him.

Sleeping on Fists

Humbly resolving to pray that God
should deliver him from evil thoughts
his head struck the ground as the woman
began hauling him along by the legs.
His uncombed head felt like one
in a bunch of fibrous coconuts
that ladies might buy along the road,
and felt also like the sting moment
his chipped Toledo blade physically
struck open one of those milk heads.
Things in fact felt here like
the state of life one imagines to exist
in the sea: wet and slow and nauseous
with the liquid soft slap after slap
undertow of waves in the insolid middle
of the seas at storm, or at wind.
But after speculation came reality.
Directly down at him her head raised
a clam and lofty eye, that exactly.
And she withdrew without lowering
even her shawl, slowly, evenly pacing,
nauseously counting out precious steps
as if measuring thereby her misfortune
along the length of the room.
But his own eyes raised then fell
as if the cords that held them taut
had been severed suddenly, he imagined,
like carrots for the evening meal,
both eyes at the same instant useless,
half-eyes, half-men.
Inside he turned sadly to himself:
This is how I embraced your mother

when against her wishes I went
fiercely to fight in the last war.
And then he sang, to answer himself,
Why do the whores all love me so?
Look at my thumb and look at my toe.

He fell drunk again, and asleep,
like all the other times of celebration,
she thought, that should have been better,
the Christmas, the New Year, the birthday.
He had whispered instead that her eyes
opened like huge and wet, ugly clams
which tried to draw his spirit
into her muscly insides
smooth and soft and disgusting
the way he said her feminine envelope
tried to swallow him up on cold nights.
But he would rather be cold than die.
This was unfair, these comments to her.
She was after all his wife, and he had
chosen her, and this was the truth.
He had measured a hard life
but so had she, harder even—she had
lived with him, had been forced
in some way inside to care.
So this was their way, she nodded.
He to be drunk, and herself
to take charge of him, to pull him
physically out of loose women
and drag him home as if he were a drunk
or a bad man after all, added to
the days he had to live with himself
and with her, her clam and salt eyes.
But these were their functions, she

decided, and all else was without meaning,
the celebration of sadness
must take this form.

The Man She Called Honey, and Married

In her hands she holds
purple blossoms inside
under her sailor-white skin
like a tattoo, like tattooes all over
of the Virgin of Guadalupe and Christ
too old now to have a face
or a body, just pieces of them now
huge on her forearms
and her face,
bigger almost
bursting out larger in some places
than the skin to hold them,
no room in her small eyes
to see more
than these purple flowers and
black and yellow,
bouquets smelling greenhouse hot inside
behind her eyes, in the pit of her head
smelling with her eyes
drawing the breath of pain
through them
into herself, into her small center
for one hard moment like a man,
a sailor, was a sailor, tattooed
and the long second he took
to put his pictures on her
with his hands.

Wet Camp

We have been here before, but we are lost.
The earth is black and the trees are bent
and broken and piled as if the game
of pick-up-sticks were ready and the children
hiding, waiting their useless turns.
The west bank of the river is burned
and the Santa Cruz has poured onto it.
The grit brown ponds
sit like dirty lilies in the black.
The afternoon is gone grazing
over the thin mountains.
The night is colder here without leaves.
Nothing holds up the sky.

The Pioneer Hotel Fire

Older, she steps out on the ledge
still pretty in a nightgown
and he sees her, up there
almost in the dinner-fork flames
she has been running to avoid
and now can't, breathless, he sees her
run over the crowd
into his secret arms,
falling at first but then turning
on her soft elbow,
propping herself up
on a comfortable couch in mid-breath
so that he can be there with her
in secret, she smiling at him,
allowing him to be falling
then on top of, allowing herself
to be taken down in an electric moment
of violation, doing what shouldn't be done
to the exciting bride of another man,
kissing and biting still breathless
she is shouting, yet not that exactly,
trying to shout but
lost in the almost and almost and
then two short single personal explosions.

Some Years

Some years people just die
and everybody says isn't it strange
almost eerie like the world
all of a sudden was haunted
like a house
but a real one, not a carnival one,
like the old Cortinas house,
and you were inside, alone
and nothing, not one thing, moved.
Then some years people just have
children, and you watch
like you watch the popcorn machines
in the theater lobbies,
in the El Dorado or the Buena Vista,
and that's how the whole thing smells
from over the counter, like popcorn,
and none of them, having popped out,
is mongoloid, and none has diabetes.
And some years nothing happens
and you don't remember them as years
so that when you look at your own
body, it looks like someone else's
and the police won't do a thing
so you have to keep what you've got
and wonder what it's really done,
and what it smells like most,
and if it's died.

The Men in Dreams

He is wearing a striped pair of pants
a little too short, white socks finishing
the distance to his creased black shoes
which set off his black plastic glasses
whose stems fit perfectly into the space
above his ears and below his hairline,
long front hair brushed back by his hands
whose nails are a little too long, dirty
black underneath like the stems of the
glasses, black like the also-creased thin
belt he wears, and has worn, that's too big
and hangs down in front, just a little,
pulled tight, making his cotton shirt fully blossom,
and wearing finally a sleeveless undershirt
here in Arizona, so he's visibly wet at the armpits.

He is a stranger, but like the odd men in dreams
so that I have seen him before, I am sure of it,
and that is how he is able to be shouting
my name before he reaches me, almost friendly.
I smell him before he comes close, clearly,
and I wait; I know this time the man is real.
I wait until he tells me something, about relatives,
about death, explaining about his being so
terminally sad; sadness like his is disease,
he says, too much for one thin man to face
because every family has had friends who have
died in some horrible way and then seen sadness
passed on to daughters, who become cousins
to each of us, from whom letters keep coming
and to whom we write back only to ask discreetly
the growing particulars of this singular disease

so that we might know it plainly when our times comes;
and it will come, more powerful even than the
horrible death which caused it, for the diseased
live on, always around us, holding out their plain
flat hands. He is infected, but happy to see me.

I wait, and learn that he is sad for me, too,
sad for anything sorrowful that might have happened
ever, that is how far his disease has gone.
I wait, and then he leaves. I have not said
a word, but the man is not upset, or he has left
so quickly I couldn't tell, and I am left wondering
like those curious moments when something is said,
or a noise made, and no one acknowledges anything.

The Man I Cannot Talk To

Food should run short.
Forgiveness will begin
to feel closer, to feel
like slippers at the side
of a large bed.
A man will begin to dream
things that will spawn
no contempt in the hearts
of decent women.
Hunger becomes for the moment
an important word
in my limited vocabulary.
Evelyn or Carol or Betsy
sends up the homemade bread
and I refuse it
because I want it,
trying to make myself hungry.
When I was younger
on a windy day in fall
a group of fieldworkers came
as they had on other days
into a tavern before dinner.
I try to relive what they
had to face going home,
my walk as I followed them,
each man strong and laughing.
To have drunk, not to be hungry
for dinner, to be yelled at,
but to have saved food.
The feeling is primal,
hunger for the wrong reasons.
Such is a man.

Silence would take over,
words at least being retained
to fill out the body.
I think of the splash of falls,
of trees, of big cities and
shopping malls, of movies.
I stop then and eat,
carefully and slowly,
eating everything and more,
realizing in one moment
that I am not those fieldworkers,
each one is a stranger,
even the one who every day
led me home from the tavern,
spoke to me, and having used
precious words thereby grew
shorter. I have felt hunger
also for the wrong reasons,
but I am not a smart enough
animal to cover my tracks
with a thin and quiet tail.

Nani

Sitting at her table, she serves
the sopa de arroz to me
instinctively, and I watch her,
the absolute *mamá*, and eat words
I might have had to say more
out of embarrassment. To speak,
now-foreign words I used to speak,
too, dribble down her mouth as she serves
me albondigas. No more
than a third are easy to me.
By the stove she does something with words
and looks at me only with her
back. I am full. I tell her
I taste the mint, and watch her speak
smiles at the stove. All my words
make her smile. Nani never serves
herself, she only watches me
with her skin, her hair. I ask for more.

I watch the *mamá* warming more
tortillas for me. I watch her
fingers in the flame for me.
Near her mouth, I see a wrinkle speak
of a man whose body serves
the ants like she serves me, then more words
from more wrinkles about children, words
about this and that, flowing more
easily from these other mouths. Each serves
as a tremendous string around her,
holding her together. They speak
nani was this and that to me
and I wonder just how much of me

will die with her, what were the words
I could have been, or was. Her insides speak
through a hundred wrinkles, now, more
than she can bear, steel around her,
shouting, then, What is this thing she serves?

She asks me if I want more.
I own no words to stop her.
Even before I speak, she serves.

Deciding on a Face

1.
I watch the black
hole of the oven
early in the morning
and I think of
the small brown faces
in black veils
on the way to church:
each face
a little blacker
with each year
until face and veil
become indistinguishable.
But the process
continues: a black veil
begins to show, becomes
suddenly obvious in a
brown face, in the space
of an open mouth,
in the nostrils viewed
by a child, in
the holes of the ears
when the hair
is tied back, in
the centers of the eyes.
The intricacies of
the lace veil become
imprinted on their
faces, on my grandmother's
face, everything
is black lace, patterned,
an expensive skin.

I watch the black
hole of the oven
as she bends
to take out
breads, praying
they are not burned,
the bend as prayer.

2.
We sit to dinner
three for manicotti,
checked cloth, white
wine, garlic bread.
We order and
no one is offended.
The waitress lights
our candle.
My father said once
during the war
he saw the sign no
dogs or mexicans
allowed but this
must not be
that place.
We eat our large
dinner, and I
wonder about that
other place, the
beautiful young girls
who ate on a patio
a dinner like
ours, who tasted
the garlic bread
in my hands.

3.

The face by which I had
known her is a lie.
The pointed blades of
her back reach out,
letting go or holding
her to the large bed,
giving the illusion
of weight.
From the bed she
extends stiffly her
arms, thin praying
extensions of a mantis
and a loud noise
makes her breathe in,
she jerks her arms back,
shivers like an animal
stupidly caught between
a door and its jamb.
In that moment she
frightens her history
out onto her body
as if the past were
a shield or the small,
creased and glove-worn
cover of a Catholic Bible,
the kind with yellow
pages like old teeth
and illuminated letters
that look like doilies,
intricate but useless,
painstakingly produced.
Last month she said
she would not have pets
when she got home

because they die
in their various ways
and she had not the
strength to bury another.
Today she has said
nothing until we are
ready to leave, she
has opened her eyes,
someone has placed her
glasses properly but has
forgotten to remove
them — they will fall when
she sleeps — she asks,
looking at me,
what is your name?

4.
Not all nuns creep
not those arthritics
with steel implanted
voluminous hips
always lopsided
making them nuns
secretly even beneath
their large skirts,
bicycle riders
out too far
without water
but coming downhill
unfunny, without
subtlety, or comfort.

5.
Pinned on his oversized lapel
an illiterate arrow pointed north.

Was this north? he asked me.
His parents had died
who were too poor to have left
anything behind except him.
Neighbors sent him now
northward to relatives
who had big rooms, they said.
A car would pick him up
if he stood next to the road
and he could explain
or perhaps the bus driver
would take pity on his size.
Neighbors had reassured him.
Regardless, I faced him now.
Yes, this is north, I said
and I watched him walk.
I would have invited him home.
He might have stayed.

Winter Along the Santa Cruz

Ground squirrels snap and turn
like the motion that spins a child's wooden top,
but the river sand is still, like heavy cream
left out too long, assuming the color
death requires, still and stretched:
severed long arm lying, crooked at its elbow,
white with the last summer pulses
of rain through its hard and thinning arteries
sucking in liquid instinctively, feeding
on itself, first from its fingers, then wrist,
taking everything in, leaving its parts dry,
the river consumes everything but the clear sweat
of its own effort, visible in the early morning,
beads carried off by the wind and the redbirds
and the sailors who are lost.

The Woman's Ears

Not with her hands
which were too heavy now
to bring to her face
or with her silver eyes
which were eyes for her
no longer
but with her ears
pierced as a child
by a lady who was a witch
she knew the careful sounds
of death.
Four times she had heard it
and held it in her hands.
It had gone
always without her
but she notices now
because she is too weak
for housework
the sounds in her stomach
which have grown louder.
She is old, she says
but not so old
she can be fooled so easily.
I hear her as
she tells her sons
soon it will be time.

La Sequía

Peaches are drying up all around
Elfrida, Arizona. I must be
like my grandfather, without a sound
to show he's worried at all; his brown
hand rubs the elbow that feels like the
peaches are drying up all around
the pores and ridges of his skin and down
his back. My father used to do that; he,
like my grandfather, without a sound
of complaint, wore a fire that was blond
on his head. He too would say, *I can see*
peaches are drying up all around
through the blue-eyes bruises he gave me
like my grandfather, without a sound
gave him one summer, one night on the ground
ripping apart the only thing he could. The
peaches are drying up all around
like my grandfather, without a sound.

Grandfather, They Say, Sang

For every one of his seven children
my grandfather, the picture, wrote a song
and sang each to each of them until, in one,
he slept too well alone on a boat,
the telegram that left his mandolin
unmentioned. He could not have known the song
of dying too soon, making widow that
which needed him, my voice, which cries I will
imagine those songs not made marrow in
me: *Norma made right Lilí, hillside white*
with graves that César put there, Alma, soul
of this, Margót, the sounds of I, I killed,
María, conscience, named like Norma, all
is right they weep to what can't hear, unborn,
and left, to be my father, Alvaro,
to tell me in words: I am foreign here,
and that the seven children confuse which
words were sung, seeing, naked, me come born
denied even the senses which choose the
only song mine: *I have lost the music.*

Sundays Visiting

No one sat in the chair
even after she died.
It was hers and had arms
like a zoo animal is fat,
arms squeezed out of the sides
with the weight of its world
like her body, like the heavy
tips of her painful smile
and the edges of her eyes
and the bent corners
of the glasses that covered them
so thick I couldn't see in
and she couldn't see me.

But I could see the picture
above her everywhere, as if it
were hung in every room;
I don't remember if the picture
was framed; it was not of my
great-grandmother, but of Our Lady
of Fatima, of two eyes so black,
yet the eyes were not themselves
important, it was that color lacking
in them: steep, ragged black
straight back without discernible
borders or end or weight,
and under those eyes, uncommon,
shoe-black freckles, holes almost,
eaten through her face, pinpricks
showing flatly absent insides,
sucking me into the cramped space

of the thin picture like the sliding
edge of the limitless well.

Así son los santos, said my great
grandmother, pointing, such are
the pictures of saints, she said, saint
or better, *angel* maybe, one of
the lower orders, but not a bad angel, *no*.
I thought later, an avenging angel,
like the Mormon boy had told me, angel
with sword and surprise, each held
in a hand just out of the picture
waiting to catch a young boy
on a high toilet seat.

Her room was the last one
in back, the very small one
that fit her like a suit, always
locked, and whose windows
had been used elsewhere.

Behind the room was the canyon
where we went to throw rocks
as if that were our business,
to kick weeds, always hard,
to be outside that house.
Nothing hung in the air,
there was nowhere to sit
but on our thin heels, nothing
closed us in or locked us out
that we couldn't kick down
like weeds with our small feet,
the words of our new language.
From there, to the left, Mexico;
right, the weeds broken, two beer cans,

Tres Equis; ahead, houses on other hills,
out of place, exposed, nowhere else
to go; and behind, the sound
of my cousin breathing obscenities
physically into the late summer wind,
September, October, whispering his words,
whispering to fool the wind
which always carries a secret farther.

Poetry from The Sheep Meadow Press

Desire for White
Allen Afterman (1991)

Early Poems
Yehuda Amichai (1983)

Travels
Yehuda Amichai (1986)

**Poems of Jerusalem and
Love Poems**
Yehuda Amichai (1992)

Father Fisheye
Peter Balakian (1979)

Sad Days of Light
Peter Balakian (1983)

Reply from Wilderness Island
Peter Balakian (1988)

5 A.M. in Beijing
Willis Barnstone (1987)

Wheat Among Bones
Mary Baron (1979)

The Secrets of the Tribe
Chana Bloch (1980)

The Past Keeps Changing
Chana Bloch (1992)

Memories of Love
Bohdan Boychuk (1989)

Brothers, I Loved You All
Hayden Carruth (1978)

Selected Poems
Diana Der-Hovanessian (1994)

Orchard Lamps
Ivan Drach (1978)

A Full Heart
Edward Field (1977)

Stars in My Eyes
Edward Field (1978)

New and Selected Poems
Edward Field (1987)

Embodiment
Arthur Gregor (1982)

Secret Citizen
Arthur Gregor (1989)

**The River Serpent and
Other Poems**
Arthur Gregor (1994)

Nightwords
Samuel Hazo (1987)

Leaving the Door Open
David Ignatow (1984)

The Flaw
Yaedi Ignatow (1983)

The Ice Lizard
Judith Johnson (1992)

The Roman Quarry
David Jones (1981)

Claims
Shirley Kaufman (1984)

Summers of Vietnam
Mary Kinzie (1990)

The Wellfleet Whale
Stanley Kunitz (1983)

The Moonlit Upper Deckerina
Naomi Lazard (1977)

Poems of B.R. Whiting
B. R. Whiting (1992)

Flogging the Czar
Robert Winner (1983)

Breakers
Ellen Wittlinger (1979)

Landlady and Tenant
Helen Wolfert (1979)

Sometimes
John Yau (1979)

Flowers of Ice
Imants Ziedonis (1987)

Other Titles from Sheep Meadow

Kabbalah and Consciousness
Allen Afterman (1992)

Collected Prose
Paul Celan (1986)

The Quilt and Other Stories
Ismat Chughtai (1994)

Dean Cuisine
Jack Greenberg and
James Vorenberg (1990)

**The Notebooks of
David Ignatow**
David Ignatow (1984)

**A Celebration for
Stanley Kunitz**
Edited by Stanley Moss (1986)

**Interviews and Encounters
with Stanley Kunitz**
Edited by Stanley Moss (1993)

The Stove and Other Stories
Jakov Lind (1983)

Two Plays
Howard Moss (1980)

Arshile Gorky
Harold Rosenberg (1985)

Literature and the Visual Arts
Edited by Mark Rudman (1989)

**The Stories and Recollections
of Umberto Saba**
Umberto Saba (1993)

No Success Like Failure
Ivan Solotaroff (1994)

**Cape Discovery: The Fine Arts
Work Center Anthology**
Bruce Smith & Catherine
Gammon, editors (1994)

The Tales of Arturo Vivante
Arturo Vivante (1990)

**Will the Morning Be Any
Kinder than the Night?**
Irving Wexler (1991)

**The Summers of James and
Annie Wright**
James and Annie Wright (1981)

DATE DUE

MAY 1 9 1999		
MAY 2 6 1999		
June 2.99		

GAYLORD   #3523PI   Printed in USA